IF I WERE A... FELINE

WRITTEN BY
CHARIS MATHER

WINDMILL BOOKS

Published in 2025 by Windmill Books,
an Imprint of Rosen Publishing
2544 Clinton St.
Buffalo, NY 14224

Written by:
Charis Mather

Edited by:
E.C. Andrews

Designed by:
Ker Ker Lee

Cataloging-in-Publication Data
Names: Mather, Charis, 1999-.
Title: Feline / Charis Mather.
Description: Buffalo, NY : Windmill Books, 2025. | Series: If I were a… | Includes glossary and index.
Identifiers: ISBN 9781538398074 (pbk.) | ISBN 9781538398081 (library bound) | ISBN 9781538398098 (ebook)
Subjects: LCSH: Felidae--Juvenile literature.
Classification: LCC QL737.C23 M376 2025 | DDC 599.75--dc23

Printed in the United States of America

CPSIA Compliance Information: Batch #CW25WM
For Further Information contact Rosen Publishing at 1-800-237-9932

Photo Credits – Images are courtesy of Shutterstock.com. With thanks to Getty Images, Thinkstock Photo and iStockphoto.

Characters – yusufdemirci. Recurring images – Sachiko Nakai. Cover – 2021 Photography, Abeselom Zerit, Mike Hewison, evrymmnt. 2–3 – Vladimir Turkenich. 4–5 – jeep2499, Tomas Hulik ARTpoint. 6–7 – Jane Biriukova, mama_mia, Narcis Virgiliu, Oleksandr Volchanskyi. 8–9 – Aldo De Rooster, Danita Delimont. 10–11 – Barbara Ash, Holly S Cannon, Ondrej Prosicky, WinWinFolly. 12–13 – Gemma Simpson, slowmotiongli. 14–15 – Poetry Photography, slowmotiongli. 16–17 – Abeselom Zerit, Danita Delimont. 18–19 – slowmotiongli. 20–21 – Dr Ajay Kumar Singh, Valanto.

CONTENTS

Words that look like this can be found in the glossary on page 24.

FABULOUS FELINES

It must be fabulous to be a feline.

A FELINE IS AN ANIMAL FROM THE CAT FAMILY.

Many felines are very strong and graceful animals. Even though felines have a lot in common, each different kind has its own characteristics that make it stand out.

If you were a feline, what would you be? Would you be small, cute, and fluffy? Or would you be big, strong, and fast? There are so many kinds of cats to choose from!

DOMESTIC CAT

Many domestic cats are happy to be looked after by humans, but they are also good at taking care of themselves. Cats can spend around half of their day licking their fur clean.

Domestic cats come in different sizes, but they are usually smaller than most wild cats. Some have short fur, some have long fur, and some have no fur at all!

LION

Lions are much bigger than domestic cats. They can scare other animals away with their loud roars. A male lion's roar can be heard from around 5 miles (8 km) away!

A group of lions is called a pride. When a pride needs food, the female lions work together to hunt.

Young lion cubs practice their hunting skills by play-fighting.

Lions are sometimes called lazy because they spend most of the day napping!

TIGER

Tigers are the largest felines in the world. Their orange and black striped bodies can be around 10 feet (3 m) long.

I would be a sneaky, stripy tiger!

Every tiger has its own unique pattern of stripes.

Tigers have white spots of fur on the backs of their ears. Their ear spots may help them silently signal other tigers behind them when they are hiding or sneaking up on prey.

These ear spots can warn tiger cubs of danger ahead.

FISHING CAT

Many felines do not like getting wet. However, fishing cats do not mind water at all. They are fantastic swimmers. They dive into the water to catch fish with their sharp teeth and claws.

Fishing cats have special fur that can keep them warm even in cold water. They have a thick layer of fur that stops cold water from reaching their skin.

CHEETAH

Cheetahs are the fastest animals on land. Some cheetahs can run at speeds of around 75 miles (120 km) per hour. That is the speed of a car on the highway!

Cheetahs' bodies are perfectly suited for running. Compared to other felines, they are very light. They have smaller heads, longer legs, and extra bendy backs that help them stretch out more when running.

Long tails help cheetahs balance and change direction while running.

SNOW LEOPARD

Snow leopards live in cold mountain areas that often get snow. Their thick fur helps keep them warm. When it gets extra cold, snow leopards wrap their fluffy tails around themselves like a scarf.

When it comes to jumping, few felines are better than snow leopards. Some have managed jumps higher than 30 feet (9 m) into the air. They can jump around 50 feet (15 m) in a straight line.

SAND CAT

Sand cats are small felines that only live in hot, dry deserts. If sand cats catch and eat enough prey, they can survive for a long time without drinking much water.

To keep themselves from getting too warm, sand cats dig **burrows** under the sand to live in. They stay in their burrows during the hottest parts of the day and come out to hunt at night.

Sand cats sometimes bury prey under the sand to eat later.

SERVAL

I would be a serval so I could have super hearing!
Compared to the rest of their bodies, servals have very large ears. When servals hunt in tall grass, they use their great hearing to figure out exactly where their prey is hiding.

Once servals have heard their prey, they wait for it to come close. Then, they leap up and take their prey by surprise. Servals can jump nearly 10 feet (3 m) into the air.

Servals sometimes eat mice and frogs.

WHAT WOULD YOU BE?

...as fast as a cheetah.
...as good at jumping as a snow leopard.
...as good at hearing as a serval.
...as good at digging as a sand cat.
What would you be?

GLOSSARY

burrows holes or tunnels dug by animals

characteristics features of a living thing that help to identify it

domestic not wild; often tamed and kept by humans

family a group of animals that have certain features in common

prey animals that are hunted by other animals for food

unique unlike anything else

INDEX